of Industry Liversidge Institution

Statements Respecting the Liversidge

Institution of Industry with the Constitution and By-Laws

of Industry Liversidge Institution

Statements Respecting the Liversidge
Institution of Industry with the Constitution and By-Laws

ISBN/EAN: 9783337816247

Printed in Europe, USA, Canada, Australia, Japan

Cover: Foto ©Andreas Hilbeck / pixelio.de

More available books at **www.hansebooks.com**

RESPECTING THE

𝔏𝔦𝔳𝔢𝔯𝔰𝔦𝔡𝔤𝔢 𝔍𝔫𝔰𝔱𝔦𝔱𝔲𝔱𝔦𝔬𝔫 𝔬𝔣 𝔍𝔫𝔡𝔲𝔰𝔱𝔯𝔶

WITH THE

CONSTITUTION AND BY-LAWS.

BOSTON, MASS., OCTOBER, 1881.

BOSTON:

PRESS OF ROCKWELL AND CHURCHILL, 39 ARCH STREET.

1881.

Liversidge Institution of Industry.

LOCATION.

The Liversidge Institution of Industry is situated on River street, between Lower Mills Village and Mattapan, Ward 24, in that part of Boston formerly called Dorchester.

GROUNDS AND BUILDINGS.

The buildings stand upon a fine elevation, commanding on the south and west a beautiful and far-reaching view of the old town of Milton, with her Blue Hills rising in the distance, and the Neponset river gliding gracefully along the foreground.

Directly east of the buildings, adjoining the highly cultivated and picturesque grounds of the Hon. John Conness, which form the eastern boundary of the estate, is a grove of ancient pines. On the north the grounds rise into a charming elevation, commanding a wide view of the surrounding country, and skirted on every side by forests, on one portion of which stands a grove of oaks of more than a century's growth; while on the west nature has deftly piled rocks upon rocks, and arranged the shade above, and the covering of moss and flowers around, and fashioned a basin for water below, as no hand of man can do.

The whole grounds embrace an area of sixty-two acres of rolling land, diversified with hills, rocks, gardens, and groves, and skirted in front along the whole line by the Neponset river; making this a most beautiful and picturesque spot, and of all others fitted for an institution of this kind, where the boys, separated from the temptations and allurements of the town, and face to face with Nature in her most attractive forms, may have before them that which shall awaken a sense of the beautiful and of the grand, leading them from Nature to Nature's God.

HISTORY OF THE CHARITY.

In the year 1829 Stephen Liversidge, an iron-merchant of Rotherham, England, with his wife and four sons, embarked for this country on board the packet ship Wm. Thompson, Captain Maxwell, and arrived in New York Aug. 19th, after a passage of thirty-three days. After exploring the country somewhat, he took up his residence in Dedham, Mass., for a short time, and then removed to Milton, boarding with his family for nearly a year at the "Atherton Tavern," now the residence of Mr. David G. Hicks; afterwards he occupied the estate of J. Smith Boies, of Milton, now owned by A. W. Austin, Esq.; and then lived for a time on the estate formerly owned by Capt. Henry Cox, on Brush Hill Turnpike, Dorchester.

In 1835 Mr. Liversidge purchased a part of the land now embraced in this charity, and soon after erected the mansion which forms a part of the Institute Building.

Here he established a manufactory of starch and gums. This business he pursued through life, with the aid of his sons, who engaged in their father's occupation, till the last one passed away.

Mr. Liversidge was a man of enterprise and of large business capacity. His business grew from a small beginning to large dimensions, and proved highly remunerative. With his increasing prosperity he retained his English habits and customs. His home was the old English mansion, open to a broad hospitality. A portion of his domain was enclosed as a deer-park. His grounds and gardens were laid out after English style, and his flowers and trees were such as were familiar in the old country.

At his decease the estate descended to his children; and afterwards, as the band of brothers diminished, it passed from one brother to another, as no one of them ever married, until the decease of Thomas, the second in age, who survived the others, and was the last of the family, and the founder of this charity.

FOUNDER OF THE CHARITY.

Thomas, the son of Stephen and Mary Liversidge, was born at Thryburg, England, Feb. 15, 1813. His life was passed mostly at Dorchester in the diligent pursuit of the business established by his father. He made several visits to England, the last of which was but a short time prior to his death, when he became greatly interested in the scenes of his childhood, and eagerly sought out and renewed early friendships.

He died at his residence in Dorchester, Jan. 14, 1876, aged 62 years 10 months and 30 days.

In the disposition of the estate by will, after legacies amounting to about forty thousand dollars to relatives and institutions in England, and to friends and religious societies in this country, he bequeathed all the residue and remainder of his property of every description to his executors and trustees, absolutely and forever, in trust, nevertheless : —

" To establish, keep, and maintain an institute to be called the ' Liversidge Institution of Industry ' ; the object and purpose of which shall be, to take and receive male children of persons who are poor and destitute, and also those boys who have lost their parents, or whose parents neglect to provide for them ; and in said Institution to fit and prepare them for some of the industrial pursuits of life, especially for the business of agriculture, and for the various branches of the mechanic arts ; the children to be received into said Institution to be between the ages of seven and fourteen, and to be taken only with the consent of their parents if living, with authority and power from them to bind them out at the age of fourteen with suitable persons till they shall arrive at the age of twenty-one years, with whom they can be taught the practical business of agriculture, or some other of the industrial pursuits of life. The children to be admitted to this Institution to be natives of England and New England only.

"My object in making this bequest is to build up and maintain **an** Institution in which boys shall be taught the value and respectability of labor, and of habits of industry, as the best and surest foundation for happiness and success in life. The details relating to the establishment, regulations, and management of this Institution I leave to the discretion and judgment of my said trustees, subject to the foregoing restrictions and conditions."

BUILDINGS ERECTED.

In accordance with the authority thus vested in them, the Trustees have caused to be erected suitable buildings for the purpose of carrying out the object of the testator, and bringing this noble charity into practical operation.

In doing this they have retained the site of the old Liversidge Mansion, using it as the south-westerly part of the Institution, and annexing thereto, north-easterly, a new building of 66 feet front and 80 feet depth, with such changes in the old building as were necessary to give architectural unity to the whole structure.

Thus the best location that the grounds afford has been secured to the Institution; and, by utilizing the old building, a cost of many thousand dollars has been saved.

The building has a total frontage of one hundred and twelve feet, with a depth of forty-two feet in the old part, and eighty feet in the new part.

It is two stories high, with tower, Mansard roof, and piazza. The new part is devoted wholly to the boys. Their dormitories, occupying the entire upper story, are light, airy, and pleasant. Their library, sitting-room, hospital, and various other rooms in the second story, finished and furnished in ash, are cheerful and attractive. On the first floor are the school-room, dining-room, kitchen, laundry, drying-room, ice-room, pantry, and china-closet; while the basement furnishes a spacious play-room, bathing-room, and various other conveniences for the boys. The Trustees have given special attention to drainage, ventilation, light, and heat, in the construction of the building. Two spacious stairways, direct and easily accessible, descend from the dormitories to the ground-floor.

The entire building is lighted by gas, is abundantly supplied with water, and is warmed by three large furnaces in the basement.

The great aim in the planning and construction of the Home has been to secure the health, safety, comfort, and happiness of those who are to occupy it.

As the founder of this benevolent enterprise designed to reach out after, and gather in those boys who had none to care for their welfare, and who had only the heritage of poverty and hardship; and to teach them the "value and respectability of labor, and of habits of industry as the best and surest foundation for happiness and success in life"; so those who have been put in charge of this enterprise now open the doors of this Christian home to such boys, and, seeking that "wisdom which is profitable to direct," design, with earnest purpose, and with the use of every available means, to train and mould them into a noble and useful Christian manhood.

And this enterprise, so great and good, they earnestly commend to the gracious protection of God, and to the friendly interest, confidence, and coöperation of all good men and women, who would fain elevate and save these neglected ones, liable to become the bane and scourge of society, and make them a blessing to themselves, to their friends, and to the world.

ELEAZER J. BISPHAM, ⎫
HORATIO N. GLOVER, ⎬ *Trustees.*
ALBERT K. TEELE, ⎭

Post-office address : —   MATTAPAN, MASS.

CONSTITUTION AND BY-LAWS.

CONSTITUTION AND BY-LAWS.

ARTICLE I.

This Institution shall be known as THE LIVERSIDGE INSTITUTION OF INDUSTRY.

ARTICLE II.

Object and Purpose.

Its object shall be to provide a home for the nurture, care, and education of orphan and destitute boys who are "natives of England and New England only," to be admitted between the ages of seven and fourteen years, either on surrender, or as boarders in part, until suitable provision can be made for them. Its system of discipline and education shall be specially adapted to the wants of the boys committed to its charge; it shall aim to be, as nearly as possible, that of a well-regulated Christian family, so as to present the strongest incentive to virtue and the most effective restraint from vice. *Its great purpose and aim shall be to train and mould the boys committed to its charge into a noble and useful Christian manhood.*

ARTICLE III.

Board of Control.

The management and control of the Institution shall be vested in a Board of Three Trustees (as provided in the will of Thomas Liversidge, its founder), appointed by Probate Court; and all vacancies shall be filled by Probate Court on the recommendation of the remaining members or member of the Board of Trustees.

ARTICLE IV.   ·

Supervision.

The Board of Trustees shall exercise a general and careful supervision over the Institution, and shall frequently and carefully inspect it in all its departments. They shall appoint and regulate the duties and salaries of Superintendent, Matron, Teacher, Farmer, and all assistants, and remove them at their discretion. They shall be the guardians of the boys (unless otherwise provided); shall procure for them suitable food, clothing, care, instruction, and employment while at the Institution, and shall transfer them to suitable trades, private families for adoption or employment, or to their relatives or friends, or to other places of abode, at the earliest period consistent with their best interests; and they shall exercise all possible care that the boys who go from the Institution receive proper and kind treatment from those to whom they are committed.

ARTICLE V.

Officers and Meetings.

The Board of Trustees shall hold stated monthly meetings on the third Wednesday of each month, at their office in the Institute Building, at 9 o'clock A.M. The meeting on the third Wednesday of January shall be the Annual Meeting, at which a President, Treasurer, Secretary, and Finance Committee of two, shall be chosen, by ballot, out of their own number, to serve for one year.

ARTICLE VI.

Officers' Duties.

The President, Treasurer, and Secretary shall perform the ordinary duties of their offices.

The Treasurer shall have the charge and care of the finances and securities, under the supervision of the Finance Committee. He shall collect, receive, and invest all moneys, and shall pay all bills, endorsed by one or more of the Finance Committee; he shall render a monthly report of receipts and expenditures, and shall prepare for Probate Court an annual account, to be presented at the annual meeting in January.

The Secretary shall keep a record of all the proceedings of the Board, have charge of all books of record and papers, and give notice of all meetings. He shall keep a register of the name and age of each boy admitted to the Institution, with the date of his admission, a sketch of his life, including his birthplace and description of his person; the name, residence, nativity, and character of his parents; with a record of his conduct while in the Institution, and as far as possible after leaving it. Whenever a boy is placed out at service he shall keep a record of the person, residence, and employment of the employer, as well as the service and terms for which he is employed. In case of his receiving notice of the ill-treatment of a boy placed out at service, it shall be his duty, at once to examine into the case, and to take such measures in reference to it as the circumstances require. He shall keep files of all letters received, and copies of all letters sent, so far as of importance for reference, in the case of each boy.

The Commitee on Finance shall supervise the financial affairs of the trust, and direct in the investment of trust funds. They shall have under their supervision all bonds, stocks, and loans. They shall examine and audit the Treasurer's accounts, and shall also audit all bills which may be incurred.

ARTICLE VII.

Superintendent.

The Superintendent shall have the general supervision of the Institution. He shall be the executive of the Trustees, and see that all their instructions and rules are

fully carried out. He shall aim to make the Institution
a well-ordered, obedient, and affectionate family. He
shall exercise a kind and fatherly discipline over the boys,
looking upon them as members of his own household; it
being understood that everything relating to their food,
clothing, manners, morals, health, recreation, study, and
labor is to be under his control, subject to the approval
of the Trustees. He is expected to win their confidence
and affection by a manifest kindly interest in their happiness and welfare, and by that principle of love that
underlies all true discipline, to draw them in the right
way. He is required to avoid corporal punishment in
every possible case; but, if it becomes absolutely necessary, a record of the time, manner, and circumstances of
such punishment is to be made. The Superintendent,
with his family, shall attend the boys at meals; he shall
invoke the divine blessing, and see that order and deco-
rum are observed at the table. He shall maintain daily
worship with the boys, and shall require them to attend
divine service once every Sabbath, at such place as the
Trustees shall provide. The Superintendent shall never
be absent from the Institution without leaving a suitable
officer in charge; and he shall not be absent during the
night without the knowledge and permission of the
Trustees. He shall not allow any child to be absent
without permission. He shall fix upon regular hours for
the children to rise in the morning and retire at night;
also hours for school, for recreation, for family, and for
farm work. He shall especially endeavor to impress
upon the children the duties and advantages of a moral
and religious, and the evils and miseries of a wicked, life;
and to inculcate all the virtues that adorn and elevate
the character.

ARTICLE VIII.

Matron.

It shall be the duty of the Matron to superintend the
internal affairs of the Institution, and, with the advice of
the Superintendent, to make arrangements respecting the

appropriate duties of the assistants. She shall preserve general order, neatness, industry, frugality, and economy; see that the food and clothes and lodging are sufficient and proper; that the boys are instructed and exercised in such branches of housework as shall be useful to them and adapted to their age and capacity; see that cleanliness, order, and propriety are maintained in all the apartments of the building, and in the person, dress and rooms of the boys; she shall exercise a maternal interest and affection over her household, and see that they have special care and every needed comfort in sickness.

ARTICLE IX.
Teacher.

The teacher shall have charge of the discipline and instruction of the school, and of the order and cleanliness of the school-room. He shall have charge of the library, and be responsible for all books and furniture in school-room and library. The studies of the school shall embrace the usual branches of Primary and Grammar Schools. The hours of school shall be arranged by the Superintendent and Trustees. The teacher, unless occupying some other position in the Institution, shall devote his time, out of school, to such duties as are needful for the prosperity and order of the Home.

ARTICLE X.
Farmer.

The farmer shall attend to the stock, take proper care of the barns and greenhouses, and, in winter, of the furnaces. Under the supervision of the Superintendent, he shall have charge of the grounds, avenues, paths, gardens, and buildings. He shall have charge of the boys in outside work; and shall instruct them in the various duties and works of agriculture and horticulture. He shall dispose of all articles raised on the farm, not needed for use; and, with his assistants, shall aim to make the farm remunerative.

ARTICLE XI.

Assistants.

All officers and assistants shall reside at the Home. None of the subordinates shall leave it without permission of the Superintendent. All persons employed in the Institution, in whatever capacity, shall be required to devote their whole attention to the performance of their duties; shall aid in maintaining the rules, and in striving to ensure the happiness and prosperity of the Home, and shall give such assistance as may be needful thereto.

ARTICLE XII.

Admission.

The Institution is designed only for boys. Boys who are orphans, or whose parents are unable to provide for their education and support, may be admitted to this Christian home. They must be between the ages of seven and fourteen; they must be natives of New England or England only; they must be free from disease of body or mind, such as would prevent them from being placed in a good Christian home. As the Institution does not partake of the nature of a school of reformation, or a hospital for the sick, or an asylum for the poor, but of a home for the boys of deserving parents, where, by the early cultivation of the mind and the right development of the moral principles, they may be saved from many temptations to a downward course, and be raised to respectability and usefulness, *therefore special regard must be had to the character and promise of the children to be received.*

The Trustees shall examine all applicants, visit the parents, or guardians, or nearest of kin, when possible; require proper papers relinquishing to the Institution all control or authority over the children, permanently or for a limited period. They shall have each child examined by a physician before admission, it being understood that no diseased candidate be received, nor any child not vaccinated at least one month previously. The Trustees, in all cases, may require a probation of a month or more before admitting to the permanent privileges of the Home.

ARTICLE XIII.

Dismission.

The boys shall be retained in the Institution until their education is fairly advanced, and their characters are in some degree developed, when they may be dismissed to other situations; provided with comfortable homes with their relatives and friends, or elsewhere; or placed, or indentured in respectable trades or occupations, as the circumstances of the case, and the judgment of the Trustees, shall determine. But the Board of Trustees shall exercise a guardianship over those who are fully given up to their protection, endeavoring to promote their prosperity and happiness until they arrive at the age of eighteen. Should any boy prove vicious and incorrigible, and decidedly injurious to the Institution, or utterly incapable of being prepared to gain a livelihood, he shall be fairly and kindly treated, and be disposed of as circumstances shall determine.

ARTICLE XIV.

Conditional Admission for a Limited Period.

Recognizing the inherent and almost universal desire, as well as the solemn obligation, on the part of parents to provide for the support and education of their children, and yet seeing in numerous cases the utter inability properly to discharge this duty, the Trustees offer the advantages of this Home, when the Institution is not filled by permanent occupants, in aid of those parents or guardians who have it in their power to meet, in whole or in part, the support of their children; requiring that a certain sum be paid per week or month, such sum being not less than one dollar per week. In such cases the parents or friends shall sign an agreement to give up the child or children entirely to the care, guardianship, and management of the Board, to be governed by the same rules and regulations as are those who are fully surrendered, so long as they remain in the family. Any responsible person who fully pays the board of a boy may withdraw him at pleasure. Boys received into the Institution as boarders shall be restored to their parents or friends at the age of twelve years, or, if remaining, be charged additional rates for board. As, however, the great object of this institution is to provide a home for orphan and destitute boys who have none to care for them, such will be considered as having a special claim to its benefits; and boys can be received as boarders only when the Home is not filled by those for whom it is specially designed.

ARTICLE XV.

Visitors.

Friends and parents of the boys shall be permitted to visit them on the last Wednesday of every month, between the hours of two and five o'clock P.M., and at no other time; but in case of sudden or severe sickness, or other pressing cause, the Superintendent may use his discretion in allowing such visits. Citizens and strangers may visit the Institution every Wednesday, between the hours of two and five o'clock P.M.

Form of a Surrender of a Boy fully given up to the Guardianship, Direction, and Management of the Institution.

KNOW ALL MEN BY THESE PRESENTS,
That I   of   in the
County of   and State of
the   of   a minor,
in consideration that the said boy has been received by The Liversidge Institution of Industry, to be nurtured,

educated, and employed according to the rules and regulations of said Institution, do hereby surrender and release the said   to the said Liversidge Institution of Industry, to the entire, sole, and exclusive care, management, and direction of the said Institution and the Board of Trustees thereof; agreeing not to interfere in any manner, directly or indirectly, with his future management or education; not to visit him at any time without the consent of the Trustees; not to interfere with, in any way, or oppose his disposal, whenever the Trustees may consider him old enough to leave the Institution; nor to ask, claim, or receive any compensation for his services, directly or indirectly, during his legal minority.

I also state that I fully understand the nature of this relinquishment; that it is my own free act and deed, made in good faith solely for the future welfare of the boy.

In token whereof I subscribe my name in the presence of witnesses this   day of   in the year of our Lord 18

Witnesses:

Form of Agreement to be signed by a Parent or Guardian who wishes to place his Boy under the Care of the Liversidge Institution of Industry, and engages to defray either in Part, or in Whole, the Expenses of the Boy.

I, the subscriber, desiring to place my son   under the care and protection of the Liversidge Institution of Industry, to be fed, instructed, and governed, agreeably to the rules and regulations of the said Institution, so long as circumstances render it necessary and expedient, do hereby agree that I will pay to the Trustees of said Institution, in consideration of the benefits that said boy will receive,   every week, or at that rate by the month; and that I will abide by all the rules and regulations of said Institution so long as said boy shall remain in said Institution; and that I will not interfere with the management or government of said boy during his residence and support in the Institution; reserving, however, the right and privilege of taking said boy out of said Institution whenever my circumstances shall render it right and consistent with the best good of the child so to do. And should I at any time apply for said boy under circumstances which, in the judgment of the Board of Trustees, will be hazardous to the morals, character, and interests of said boy, I do hereby engage and agree to abide by the judgment, decision, and advice of said Board of Trustees; and to wait until they may see that it is suitable and proper to return him to my care and protection. In case of failure to comply with the above, I hereby agree that said Institution shall assume the care of said boy and regard him as fully surrendered.

In testimony whereof I hereunto set my hand this   day of   in the year of our Lord one thousand eight hundred and

Signed in the presence of

Physician's Certificate.

LIVERSIDGE INSTITUTION OF INDUSTRY,

Boston,   18

This may certify that I have this day examined   and find him a suitable subject of admission to the Institution.

M.D.
Examining Physician.

Form of a Bequest to the Institution.

I give and bequeath to the Liversidge Institution of Industry the sum of   dollars for the use and benefit of said Institution, to be applied by the Trustees thereof to its general objects.

www.ingramcontent.com/pod-product-compliance
Lightning Source LLC
Chambersburg PA
CBHW021610270326
41931CB00009B/1415